NATURAL DISASTERS

FOREST FIRES

Luke Thompson

HIGH
interest
books

Children's Press
A Division of Grolier Publishing
New York / London / Hong Kong / Sydney
Danbury, Connecticut

Book Design: MaryJane Wojciechowski
Contributing Editors: Jennifer Ceaser and Rob Kirkpatrick

Photo Credits: Cover © Index Stock Imagery; pp. 4, 5 © Reuters/Graig Rubadoux/Archive Photos; p. 7 © Bettmann/Corbis; pp. 8, 9 © Wolfgang Kaehler/Corbis; pp. 11, 15, 21 © Raymond Gehman/Corbis; p. 12 © Craig Aurness/Corbis; p. 16 © Adam Woolfitt/Corbis; pp. 18, 19 © Christine Osborne/Corbis; p. 23 © A. T. Willett/Image Bank; pp. 24, 25 © Jonathan Blair/Corbis; p. 27 © Kirk Anderson/International Stock; p. 29 © Reuters/Gary Hershorn/Archive Photos; p. 31 © Bob Firth/International Stock; p. 32 © Charles O'Rear/Corbis; p. 35 © Michael S. Yamashita/Corbis; p. 37 © Corbis

Visit Children's Press on the Internet at:
http://publishing.grolier.com

Library of Congress Cataloging-in-Publication Data

Thompson, Luke.
    Forest fires / by Luke Thompson.
        p. cm. – (Natural disasters)
    Includes bibliographical references and index.
    ISBN 0-516-23370-X (lib. bdg.) – ISBN 0-516-23570-2 (pbk.)
    1. Forest fires—Juvenile literature. [1.Forest fires. 2. Fires.] I. Title.

SD421.23.T56 2000
634.9'618—dc21

                                                    00-028049

CONTENTS

In 1998, Florida was suffering through a drought (a long period with little or no rain). The state also was experiencing record-setting high temperatures. On May 25, because of these weather conditions, many fires broke out in Florida's forests and wilderness areas. These large, uncontrollable fires—called wildfires or forest fires—continued throughout the summer. By the end of July, 2,282 fires raged throughout the state. Florida did not have the resources to handle these blazes. Ten thousand firefighters and emergency workers from forty-seven states were called in to help control the fires.

By the end of the summer, the raging wildfires were finally under control. In those few months, however, almost 500,000 acres (200,000 hectares) of

Forest fires raged throughout Florida during the drought of 1998.

Florida's forests had been destroyed. It cost more than $130 million to fight the fires. Almost $300 million worth of timber had gone up in smoke.

A wildfire is one of the most deadly disasters known to humans. Worldwide, wildfires burn more than 12 million acres (4.8 million hectares) of forest, brush, and grassland. In the United States, an average of 110,000 wildfires burn 3.5 million acres (1.4 million hectares) every year. The United States spends about $1 billion annually to fight these fires.

Wildfires result in the loss of human and animal life, homes, and property. The smoke and haze from these fires also cause widespread pollution, which results in respiratory (breathing) problems and other illnesses.

The United States spends about $1 billion each year to fight wildfires.

CHAPTER ONE

HOW FOREST FIRES START

The Kutai National Park in Indonesia is home to one of Earth's largest rain forests. For local timber companies, Kutai is an excellent source of wood. These companies cut trees and set them on fire—a method known as slash and burn. Slash and burn is the fastest and cheapest way to clear the land so that crops can be planted. It also is a very dangerous method because the fires can easily burn out of control.

During the spring and summer of 1997, fires raged through Kutai's rain forest, destroying more than 700,000 acres (280,000 hectares). Many of the forest's animals, including an endangered species of orangutan, were killed in the blazes or were burned out of their homes.

In August, heavy rains fell on the area, but the jungle floor continued to smolder. Swamps burned, and a thick haze of smoke hung over what was left of the rain forest. At the height

...erson is practicing the dangerous technique called slash and burn.

of the enormous blaze, smoke hovered in the skies over six nearby countries. By September, the jungle—usually filled with shrieking birds, buzzing insects, and howling monkeys—was strangely quiet. Environmentalists think it may take up to 100 years for Kutai's rain forest to recover its health and beauty.

HUMANS AND FIRE

Humans are responsible for four out of every five forest fires—about 80 percent. Small actions—such as dropping a cigarette on the ground or not putting out a campfire properly—can lead to terrible forest fires. In fact, the tiniest spark or burning ember can cause a raging forest fire.

Some fires are started on purpose, to clear land for development or farming. Farmers or companies that are clearing land start about 500 million forest fires each year. Any fire that isn't started by natural sources is considered to

Some forest fires are started on purpose to clear land for development.

be a human-caused fire. For example, imagine that a telephone pole falls and an electrical spark starts a fire in the nearby woods. This is considered to be a human-caused fire, even though there weren't any people present when it happened.

Lightning is responsible for about 1 percent of all forest fires.

FIRE FROM ABOVE

The other 20 percent of forest fires are the result of natural causes. Natural fires have been occurring on Earth for millions of years. The leading cause of natural forest fires is lightning. Lightning can start a fire in a dry forest very easily. Lightning storms produce several bolts of lightning. Some of those bolts hit the ground. The intense heat and energy in a lightning bolt can cause a fire. If conditions in the forest are extremely dry, a lightning storm can start hundreds of different fires in a single forest. Each day, lightning strikes eight million times around the world. Yet only about 1 percent (80,000) of these lightning strikes cause forest fires.

A small number of wildfires are caused by other natural occurrences, such as erupting volcanoes. Hot lava and burning ash can come into contact with trees and brush, touching off a fire.

HOW DOES A FOREST FIRE BEGIN?

All a fire really needs is fuel, air, and heat. If there is a lot of fuel, if the heat is high, and if the wind is blowing, fire conditions exist. These three elements are known as the fire triangle. There has to be just the right balance of fuel, air, and heat for a fire to occur.

Fuel

The fuel part of the triangle is provided by a forest's timber. Trees—especially dead or dying ones—are forms of timber. Timber also can include dead or dry leaves and logs, twigs, small shrubs, and grass. The more fuel, the larger the fire. The larger the fire, the more heat that is produced. The more heat, the greater the potential for a large fire.

Air

Air is one of the three main ingredients that make up fire. Along with heat and fuel, every fire needs oxygen, which is provided by air. Wind feeds a fire with extra oxygen. The more oxygen that a fire takes in, the hotter it gets. The size, speed, and energy of a fire depend on how hard the wind blows. The areas of the world that suffer the worst damage from fire are often places where the wind blows the strongest.

This dying tree is considered fuel for a forest fire.

Wind does more than feed a fire with oxygen—it also helps the fire to spread. As a fire travels, it finds more fuel to burn. The more fuel it finds, the stronger it grows. If there isn't any wind to move the fire, it will eventually burn itself out. A fire needs to move to stay alive. If winds are strong enough, a fire can be pushed forward at speeds of more than 10 miles (16 km) per hour. A fire traveling at high speeds is extremely dangerous. There is no

The sun creates dry conditions that can lead to forest fires.

way to tell where it is headed. The wind that is driving the fire can shift at any moment. Shifting winds can send the fire roaring in any direction.

Heat

Sun and high temperatures dry out timber and grass. When wood and grass are dry, they burn very quickly. Fire will spread quickly over dry forest areas.

Fires that are very hot create their own wind. Hot air rises inside the fire, and cooler, fresh air rushes in to replace this rising air. This movement of air produces wind. This wind brings more oxygen to the fire, causing it to become even larger.

DID YOU KNOW?

Summer is the time during which the weather is most likely to create forest-fire conditions. In rare cases, forest fires can spring up purely because of heat. High temperatures, dry conditions, and lack of rain can cause a forest to ignite just from the heat of the sun.

Rising hot air also carries with it small pieces of burning fuel, called embers. These embers can ignite the ground in front of the main fire, causing small fires to start.

CHAPTER TWO

ELEMENTS OF A FOREST FIRE

In 1997, dry air, high temperatures, and droughts visited many parts of the world. These were ideal conditions for forest fires to start and spread out of control. More fires burned in 1997 than in any other year, which resulted in the loss of almost 12.5 million acres (5 million hectares) of forest worldwide.

Countries in South America were some of the hardest hit. About 5 million acres (2 million hectares) of land in Brazil were destroyed. Colombia was struck by 7,000 forest fires, which destroyed 42,000 acres (16,800 hectares) of national parkland. Major fires also consumed forests and grasslands in Europe, Africa, and Australia.

The aftereffects of the forest fires were devastating. Many countries in Southeast Asia suffered from severe air pollution caused by the burning forests. More than 40,000 people

The Australian Outback was destroyed by the fires of 1997.

were hospitalized with respiratory diseases as a result of smog. The smog remained in the air for months after the fires had been put out. Almost 5 million acres (2 million hectares) of land in Southeast Asia were destroyed in 1997.

THE THREE KINDS OF FOREST FIRES

All forest fires fall into at least one of three categories: ground fire, surface fire, or crown fire. Actually, a single forest fire can be all three. It can start out as a ground fire, turn into a surface fire, and eventually become a crown fire. A lot of forest fires grow in this pattern.

Ground Fire

A ground fire is a sneaky fire that can't always be seen. It does not look like a normal fire. Ground fires rarely show flames. You could walk right over a ground fire and not realize it. The only sure sign of a ground fire is the heat it creates, but unless you are walking barefoot,

When a ground fire starts showing flames, it can become a more serious surface fire.

you probably won't be aware of it. Ground fires travel low to the ground and sometimes underneath the ground. They feed on dead grass, moss, small twigs, and dry leaves.

Surface Fire

Ground fires can turn into more serious fires. A ground fire becomes a surface fire when it starts to show flames and when embers catch onto larger branches and small trees. A surface fire spreads itself along the ground, staying low but growing hot enough to burn a large amount of trees and brush.

Crown Fire

When a surface fire grows very fierce, it becomes the worst kind of forest fire—a crown fire. All of the major forest fires you hear about are crown fires. A crown fire is a fire that has grown as tall as the trees themselves. Rising heat and strong winds carry flames from treetop to treetop, causing forest fires to rage out of control. Crown fires can travel from tree to tree as fast as 10 miles (16 km) per hour. Flames can reach as high as 300 feet (91 m). Winds created by a crown fire can reach 120 miles (193 km) per hour. Columns of smoke from the fires can rise as high as 400 feet (121 m) into the air.

DID YOU KNOW?

Scientists think that ground fires from the 1983 Great Fire of Borneo (in Indonesia) are still burning today.

Flames in a crown fire travel from treetop to treetop.

CHAPTER THREE

FEARING FIRES, FIGHTING FIRES

Forest fires happen quite often in Yellowstone National Park, located in the northwest corner of Wyoming. Until 1988, the largest fire recorded in the park covered 25,000 acres (10,000 hectares). In the summer of that year, 250 fires ended up burning almost forty times that amount.

By early July, the fires had been burning for more than a month, and there was still no sign of rain. More than 200,000 acres (80,000 hectares) of evergreen forest had already burned—more than any nature expert believed possible.

The turn for the worse came on July 14. Winds of 80 miles (129 km) per hour swept across Yellowstone. The fires were given new strength by the wind. Roaring fires touched off throughout the park. Yellowstone was declared an emergency zone. Park visitors were ordered

In 1988, fires burned more than 1 million acres (400,000 hectares) of forest in Yellowstone National Park.

to evacuate (leave) the area. About 25,000 firefighters were rushed in from all over the United States to try to stop the fires.

One firefighter described his experience: "As the wind swept through the forest, the fire grew even hotter. It felt like someone had lit a match to gasoline. The forest was engulfed in flame, and I was choking on the thick, black smoke that swirled all around me."

Rain and an early snowfall finally came to Yellowstone on September 11. By then, more than 1 million acres (400,000 hectares) in and around the park had burned. It cost taxpayers $120 million to fight the fire—the park's annual budget was $17.5 million. Luckily, no one was killed in the blazes.

FIRE IN THE UNITED STATES

The western part of the United States has always experienced more forest fires than the rest of the country. States such as Colorado,

Forest fires occur often in the western part of the United States.

Idaho, Montana, Washington, and Wyoming have large amounts of forestland. In these areas, fires can blaze for weeks and destroy thousands of acres of forest.

California also has a big problem with forest fires. As the population of California grows larger every year, more people build homes in areas near forests. Several California communities already sit in the path of danger. One fire in 1977 burned down two hundred homes in the small city of Santa Barbara. In 1999, seven thousand wildfires throughout the state burned at least 275,000 acres (110,000 hectares). Wildfires destroy an average of seven hundred homes every year in California. The state spends approximately $165 million each year to repair or rebuild homes lost to wildfires.

PUTTING OUT FIRES

Fighting forest fires is not an easy task. The best weapon against any fire is, of course, water. Cold water is an especially powerful tool against fire. Cold water works in two ways to put out a blaze. First, it cools the area of the fire. Then, it snuffs out the flames.

The problem with fighting forest fires with water is getting the water to the fire. Water is

Firefighters use water to fight forest fires.

very heavy. To carry just 100 gallons (379 liters) of water takes a powerful vehicle. Fire trucks can carry large amounts of water, but there aren't always roads deep in a forest where a fire is burning. Often, firefighters must use different methods to put out fires.

Air Power

Airplanes and helicopters are very effective tools to help stop forest fires. Special planes and helicopters sweep over a large body of water, such as a lake or pond, and scoop up water into their fuselages (cargo holds). Then, they fly over the fire and dump the water. The water falls on the fire as if it were rain and puts out the blaze.

Helicopters are especially effective in fighting fires. They can hover over a fire and drop water in specific areas. Some helicopters can drop up to 2,500 gallons (9,475 liters) at a time.

Fire Lines

Sometimes, firefighters cannot put out a fire—their only hope is to contain it. They will clear out all the leaves, brush, and anything else that will act as fuel for the oncoming fire. Once this fuel is removed, firefighters dig a ditch to trap the fire and keep it from moving across

To put out a forest fire, a helicopter dumps water over the burning area.

This airplane sprays fire retardant over a large area to help prevent fire.

the forest floor. This ditch is called a fire line. Firefighters work under difficult conditions to get a fire line set up before the fire reaches the area. They must work quickly, often in hot, smoky conditions.

Fire lines depend on the fire continuing in the same direction. If the fire changes direction, the fire line will not be effective.

Fire Retardants

Fire retardants are chemical substances that help to prevent fire. The chemicals come in a form that can be sprayed, similar to the foam inside a fire extinguisher. The chemicals coat the fuel sources (such as grass and dry wood) and prevent them from catching fire.

Extreme Fire Fighting

The most exciting method of fighting forest fires is smoke jumping. The United States Department of Agriculture (U.S.D.A.) Forest Service started using smoke jumpers in 1940. Smoke jumpers fight dozens of raging forest fires each year, saving lives and homes. These men and women must be highly trained and very brave. There are only 450 smoke jumpers in the world.

Smoke jumpers are trained to parachute out of airplanes into forests. Fire-fighting supplies also are sent down by parachute. Large trunks of equipment—water pumps, tanks, hoses, axes, and shovels—land in the same area as the jumpers. The jumpers land ahead of the fire's path and use these tools to build a fire line.

A big risk in smoke jumping is landing in the wrong place. Smoke jumpers are trained to avoid landing too close to a fire. They take into consideration which direction the wind is blowing before they jump out of the plane. A person called a spotter jumps first. The spotter tries to find the best jumping spot for the whole division. He or she jumps early and tests out the wind. Once the spotter has landed, he or she then signals the rest of the crew to jump.

Another danger that smoke jumpers face is the possibility that a fire will suddenly speed up. With strong wind gusts, a fire can travel up to 10 miles (16 km) per hour—faster than a human being can run. In 1949, a tragedy occurred when a racing fire in Mann Gulch, Montana, trapped a division of smoke jumpers.

Smoke jumpers parachute into forests to fight fires.

Twelve jumpers and one forest ranger died in the blaze.

FIRE TECHNOLOGY

In the past forty years, several new advances have been made to detect forest fires. Much of this technology is very expensive, but it is also very effective. It can help get firefighters to the scene of a wildfire much more quickly, when the fires are smaller and easier to fight.

Infrared Technology

In 1966, the U.S. Forest Service started using infrared scanners to fight forest fires. Infrared scanners are devices that sense light rays giving off heat of more than 600 degrees

Fahrenheit (315 degrees Celsius). Infrared scanners can be mounted onto airplanes or helicopters. The scanners locate the most intense areas of a fire, known as hot spots. Then firefighters know where to concentrate their efforts.

Satellites

Over the past few years, satellites (space vehicles that circle Earth) have been used to help fight forest fires. The European Space Agency has developed a strategy that gives firefighters a great advantage over the fire. A satellite system takes pictures of a fire. Then, the satellite sends video images of the fire back to Earth. Using these video images, firefighters can pinpoint a fire's location and the direction in which the fire is headed. In the future, satellites will play an even bigger role in fighting forest fires. Modern satellite systems can detect even the smallest fires—those that are only 1 to 2 acres (.4 to .8 hectares) in size. These advanced satellites can spot fires before they start burning out of control.

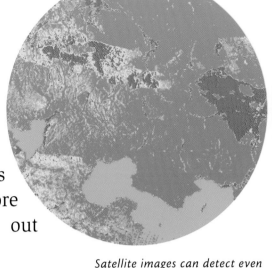

Satellite images can detect even the smallest forest fire.

Remote Automated Weather Stations (RAWS)

Special instruments called remote automated weather stations (RAWS) collect information about weather conditions. There are about 1,150 RAWS in the United States. Most of them are in the western states, where forest fires are more common. Every hour, RAWS transmit data to a satellite, which sends the information to the National Interagency Fire Center in Boise, Idaho. The Center then lets firefighters and park officials know if fire conditions exist in their area.

FRIENDLY FIRE

Everybody knows that forest fires can be very destructive. However, what many people do not know is that forest fires also are a necessary part of the cycle of life. In fact, life couldn't exist on this planet if it weren't for forest fires. Fire is as necessary to maintain Earth's ecosystem as is water. An ecosystem is the environment, including plants and animals that help to maintain it. Natural fires do a lot of good. Forest fires recycle nutrients in the soil and fight weeds. Fires help to support fish and wildlife habitats. They also help certain trees to reproduce.

DID YOU KNOW?

The terrain (features of the land) has an effect on the way fire will travel. Unlike most objects, fire moves faster uphill than it does downhill. Studying the terrain may help scientists predict the direction in which a fire will travel.

FIRE PREVENTION AND SAFETY

Because humans cause the majority of forest fires, it is necessary to use caution in wilderness areas. The following are some tips to prevent forest fires:

• When you camp, surround any fire that you build with a pile of dirt or rocks.

• Never assume a campfire is out just because you do not see any flames.

• Always dump several gallons of water onto your campfire before you leave.

• Never drop a match or cigarette on the ground, even if it looks as if it has gone out.

• If you ever catch on fire, remember to "stop, drop, and roll." By rolling on the ground, you will put out the fire.

• If you see someone who is on fire, tell him or her to drop to the ground. Then, pour water on the person or cover him or her with a blanket. The blanket will smother the flames.

Fact Sheet ●●●●●●●●

GREENLAND

NORTH
AMERICA

NORTH
ATLANTIC
OCEAN

1988
Yellowstone
National Park
1 million acres
(400,000 hectares)
burned

1998
Florida
500,000 acres
(200,000 hectares)
destroyed

1997
Colombia
42,000 acres
(16,800 hectares)
destroyed

SOUTH
AMERICA

PACIFIC OCEAN

1997
Brazil
5 million acres
(2 million hectares)
destroyed

SOUTH
ATLANTIC
OCEAN

The fire symbols show the locations of
forest fires mentioned in this book.

Forest Fires

EUROPE

ASIA

AFRICA

AUSTRALIA

1997
Kutai National Park
700,000 acres
(280,000 hectares)
burned

crown fire the largest form of forest fire; it travels from treetop to treetop

drought dry spell suffered by an area when hardly any rain falls over a long period of time

ecosystem the full cycle in which a natural environment is maintained

ember small piece of burning material that is hot enough to start a forest fire

evacuate leave for safety reasons

fire line line made by firefighters to stop a fire's forward progress

fire retardant chemical substance that helps prevent fires

fuel anything that helps a fire to burn, such as timber, leaves, and grass

fuselage the space inside an airplane where cargo is stored

ground fire a fire that travels low to the ground or underground and rarely shows flames

hot spot the most intense part of a fire

NEW WORDS

infrared having to do with light rays that give off heat

respiratory having to do with breathing or the lungs

satellite a vehicle that circles Earth in space

slash and burn method of clearing forests for development by setting the forest on fire

smoke jumper firefighter who parachutes from a plane into a burning forest

spotter the lead smoke jumper who jumps alone and then signals the others when to jump

surface fire a type of fire that forms when sparks or embers start fires on large branches and small trees

timber any substance—such as dead trees, dead or dry leaves, logs, twigs, small shrubs, and grass—that serves as fuel for fire

wildfire a widespread, uncontrolled fire that burns forest, grassland, and brush

Armbruster, Ann. *Wildfires*. Danbury, CT: Franklin Watts, 1996.

Lampton, Christopher. *Forest Fire*. Brookfield, CT: Millbrook Press, 1994.

Lauber, Patricia. *Summer of Fire: Yellowstone 1998*. New York: Orchard Books, 1991.

Magnuson-Beil, Karen. *Fire in Their Eyes: Wildfires and the People Who Fight Them*. San Diego: Harcourt Brace & Company, 1999.

Merrick, Patrick. *Forest Fires*. Chanhassen, MN: The Child's World, Incorporated, 1997.

Patent, Dorothy Hinshaw. *Fire: Friend or Foe*. New York: Clarion Books, 1998.

Pringle, Laurence P. *Fire in the Forest: A Cycle of Growth and Renewal*. Old Tappan, NJ: Simon & Schuster Children's, 1995.

Canadian Interagency Forest Fire Centre
210-301 Weston Street
Winnipeg MB Canada R3E 3H4
Web site: *www.ciffc.ca*
The Canadian Interagency Forest Fire Centre is a nonprofit corporation that provides services to help improve forest fire management in Canada. The site features FireWire, a service that gives daily updates during forest fire season.

Disasters of Nature
http://library.thinkquest.org/25019
This Thinkquest site provides a lot of information about various natural disasters, including forest fires. Find out how forest fires are started, the different types of forest fires, and the effects of these fires. This site also features a game and a quiz to help you learn more about forest fires.

RESOURCES

Smokey Bear

www.smokeybear.com

This is the official site of Smokey the Bear. It provides information about forest fires, including how they start, how much damage they can do, and how firefighters put out forest fires. Check out the games and links to learn more about preventing forest fires.

United States Fire Service—Fire News

www.fs.fed.us/fire/news.shtml

This site provides up-to-date information about recent forest fires. It also contains useful information about fire-related issues. Check back at this site often to stay on top of the current forest fire news.

INDEX

INDEX

ABOUT THE AUTHOR

Luke Thompson was born in Delaware. He holds a degree in English literature from James Madison University. He lives in Vail, Colorado.